The Missing Coin

Illustrations by Derek Matthews

CHRISTIAN FOCUS PUBLICATIONS

Jesus told a story.

'A woman had ten silver coins.'

Each one was worth about
one day's pay.

One day, disaster struck.
A coin went missing.

The woman lit her lamp...

and took a broom...

'Swish, swish,' she swept the house.

She searched the floor, and
under the furniture...

...in every crack and corner...

until, 'hooray!' she found it!

'I must celebrate,' declared the woman.

So she called together friends
and neighbours.

'Be happy with me,' she cried joyfully.

'I have found my lost coin!'

'Let me tell you,' said Jesus. 'In the same way, the angels are filled with joy when one person turns away from wrong and finds God.'

This story can be found in the Bible in Luke 15:8-10